This book belongs to

Walt Disney®

VOLUME 15

RIDE, FLOAT, AND FLY

WALT DISNEY FUN-TO-LEARN LIBRARY

One Saturday morning, Mickey woke up bright and early. It was a very special day. He had promised to meet Minnie at the train station and take her for a ride in the country in his new sports car. He'd been hoping all week it wouldn't rain.

He looked through the garage window and up at the sky. The sun was shining. It was a perfect day!

Mickey packed a picnic lunch and put it on the backseat. Then he checked under the hood to make sure the car's engine was working properly. He knew the gas tank was full because he had filled it up at the gas station the night before.

Pluto wagged his tail hopefully.

"Sorry, Pluto," said Mickey. "Maybe you can come next time."

As Mickey drove down his street, he saw lots of people going places and doing things. The mail carrier wheeled her cart from house to house delivering mail. A huge moving van was parked in front of his new neighbor's house, and the movers were unloading furniture from it.

A telephone repair truck was parked near the telephone pole, and Mickey could see the repairman taking out his tools so he could fix the wires.

By the curb, the driver of a tow truck had hitched up a banged-up car.

"Good morning!" Mickey shouted.

"To you, too," said the driver.

Mickey turned the corner onto Main Street, which was crowded with buses and cars. The buses were so big they made Mickey's sports car look tiny! One bus was pulling up at the bus stop, and a man was running to catch it. As Mickey slowed down to avoid workers paving the road, a huge tour bus pulled up behind him. Was it headed to the zoo? Or to the ocean? Mickey wondered.

Then Mickey heard the *clickety click, clickety click* of a streetcar. The streetcar ran on special tracks that were set right into the road, and when its wheels went around and around, they clicked against the rails. The conductor had a bell that he rang to let people know the trolley was on its way. *Clang, clang, clang!* it went. *Clang, clang, clang!*

All of a sudden, Mickey heard a louder sound than the streetcar. Sirens! Cars and buses moved to the side of the road to let the emergency vehicles pass. A little red car with a red bubble on top zoomed by with the fire chief in it. A big fire engine followed, carrying ladders, hoses, and fire fighters.

An ambulance rushed by with a police car on one side. The lights on the police car flashed around and around.

In the next minute, the firetruck, the police car, and the ambulance were gone!

Meanwhile, Minnie had set off to meet
Mickey. She took a taxicab to the train
station. It was a big yellow taxi with fold-up seats for extra passengers.

The driver pulled up at the station as a long freight train chugged
slowly by. It had boxcars carrying grain, open flatcars piled with logs,
and round tank cars filled with milk. Up front was the locomotive where
the engineer sat and drove the train. At the end was the caboose.

Other boxcars stood empty on the sidings. A small steam locomotive
was moving them around the busy junction. The signal changed to let
the freight train through the station.

Minnie checked the train schedule and bought her ticket. Hers would be the next train to enter the station. When the long freight train was just a speck in the distance, she heard the *toot, toot* of a train whistle. The passenger train had arrived.

The diesel engine pulled the coach cars and the special dining car into the station. "All aboard!" the conductor called.

When Minnie had found a seat in the coach car, the conductor came to punch her ticket. "Next stop is yours, ma'am," he said.

And when Minnie got off at Alexander Station, who do you think she saw waiting for her?

"We'll have plenty to eat," said Minnie, laughing. "But where are we going to have our picnic?"

"That's a surprise," replied Mickey. "Just wait and see."

It was a busy afternoon, out on the highway. On one side of the road, a big trailer truck was bringing new cars from the factory into town.

A pickup truck, with its empty milk containers clanking in the back, drove slowly home to Farmer John's farm.

A tank truck driver pulled his whistle as he sped down the highway. And there, on the side of the road, was a huge cement mixer with a drum full of fresh cement — and a flat tire.

"Need a hand changing it?" called out Mickey as he stopped to help.

"Yes, thank you," said the truck driver. "It's a lot of work for just one person."

"Well, here we are," said Mickey, when they had finally reached Hawk Mountain. "We're going to take a ride in a cable car!"

During the winter, skiers rode up the steep mountain in the little cable car that hung from a thick steel rope. Then they skied down the hill themselves. In the summer, people rode up and down the mountain in the cable car, just for the fun of it.

And for the view!

The picnic was a great success, even though Mickey and Minnie had an unexpected guest.

"What a wonderful picnic, *and* a wonderful ride," said Minnie, as they drove home on the highway. "It was a perfect day."

Just then, a car pulled up next to them, and all of its passengers began to wave.

"It's Donald Duck, Huey, Dewey, and Louie," Mickey said, as he waved back. "I wonder where they're going!"

Mickey wasn't the only one wondering where Donald, Huey, Dewey, and Louie were going. Huey, Dewey, and Louie were wondering, too! Donald was being very mysterious about where they were going on their summer vacation.

Donald drove down the road that led to Fisherman's Harbor. When they saw the boats docked in the bay, he pointed and shouted, "There it is! Our home for the summer."

Huey, Dewey, and Louie looked at each other. "Maybe it's a cruise on an ocean liner," Huey said, hopefully.

"Or a sailboat trip," said Dewey, excitedly.

"Wrong!" said Donald, leading them to a square, flat-topped boat that was tied to the dock. "We're going to live on a houseboat!"

"Come along, boys," said Donald. "Ahoy there, all aboard!"

"Aw, Uncle Donald, do we have to?" asked Dewey.

"That old boat doesn't even look as if it will float," said Louie.

"Sure it will," replied Donald, as he led the boys up the gangplank to the deck of the *Daisy D*.

While Donald looked at the charts, maps, and instructions for sailing the *Daisy D*, the three boys looked at the other boats in the bay.

Louie liked the brightly colored sailboats anchored in the harbor.
Each had its own rowboat for bringing passengers to and from the shore.
But Huey liked the big, wide fishing boats the best of all. Their huge
fishing nets were drying in the sun.

As the *Daisy D* moved out of the harbor, a tugboat chugged by, pushing a big ship out to sea. The driver waved and pulled the whistle. *Toot, toot!*

The Sun Island ferry waited for the *Daisy D* to pass before setting out to cross the bay. There were people, dogs, and bicycles—as well as cars—taking the ferry ride to Sun Island. Donald, Huey, Dewey, and Louie had taken it once, too.

The *Daisy D* chugged across the harbor and around the bay, under the direction of proud Captain Donald.

As night fell over the water, Donald and the nephews stopped the engine and caught fresh fish for dinner. A police boat cruised by. A Coast Guard cutter came in to rest for the night. Some fishermen untied their boats and headed out to sea for a little night fishing.

The *Daisy D's* crew watched the moon rise, and then they fell asleep.

The next morning, Donald woke to a big surprise.

"We forgot to drop the anchor to keep the boat in one place," Huey whispered to him. "And look where we drifted during the night."

"Wow," Donald said. "That's a military naval base."

They could even see a huge, gray aircraft carrier, a ship so big it had a runway for planes to land on. Circling around were PT boats, guarding the harbor. Donald felt very small.

Suddenly, something big and gray began rising out of the water. "Yipes," said Donald. "Here comes a whale!"

But it wasn't a whale. It was a submarine, a special kind of boat that can stay underwater for a long time, and then come up again. The crew of this submarine had come up to look at the curious boat it had seen from down below—and that boat was Donald's!

The captain shouted and waved as Donald turned the *Daisy D* around and chugged back to the bay.

A few days later, Donald was sunbathing on deck when he saw a big, beautiful yacht pull up next to the houseboat. The yacht had two tall masts. Its three sails flapped in the wind. There was even a big cabin beneath the deck, where the crew could sleep.

The yacht's captain shouted, "Ahoy!" When Donald saw who it was, his eyes grew as round as saucers.

UNCLE SCROOGE!

"Mind if I join the fun?" Scrooge asked, and then added, "Or better yet, why not join me!"

Huey, Dewey, and Louie took turns riding Scrooge's wind surfboard. Huey held on tight as he bounced over the waves.

Donald tried to water-ski, but his legs didn't seem to understand what they were supposed to do!

A week later, the crew turned the *Daisy D* around and headed back along the bay to Fisherman's Harbor. They were sorry they had to go home. How they'd loved the life at sea!

Then suddenly, Donald heard people cheering. When he looked around, he saw some very strange boats in the water, and they seemed to be racing. There were canoes and kayaks, bumping into each other. Someone was driving a small boat with propellers. Someone else was floating in an old bathtub.

"Why, it's THE GREAT RACE!" shouted Donald. "Anyone can enter this race, in anything that floats. Let's join in."

Donald and the nephews worked so hard, they won a special prize!
It was a great way to end a perfect holiday.

"That sure looks like fun," Goofy thought when he saw Donald in the Great Race. "But I'm glad I'm here!"

Goofy was taking his very first plane ride. He was sitting next to the pilot in the cockpit of a two-seater "prop" plane. In front of them was a big board full of things to push and pull to make the plane fly. Special clocks told them how high they were flying and how fast they were going. The propeller on the nose of the plane turned around and around. It was very exciting.

The little prop plane was part of the County Air Fair held near Goofy's home. It was the first plane he'd seen when he arrived at the fair. But it was only one of the many kinds of planes at the fair, and when Goofy looked around him, he saw some others.

Below him was a seaplane, which had floats instead of wheels so it could land in the water.

Above him was a snowplane, with skis instead of wheels, so it could come down in the snow. Goofy thought that one looked like lots of fun.

Some of the little planes were called gliders. They flew without engines. A prop plane helped lift them up off the ground. Then, once in the air, they rode silently and gently on the power of the wind.

Goofy took a helicopter ride at the fair, too. The helicopter flew without wings! But it did have a propeller on the roof that whirled around and around very fast. The propeller lifted the helicopter up, and brought it back down again, too. The helicopter could fly straight up and down (which planes can't do), as well as forward and backward. And it could stay still in the air without moving at all!

A small, noisy plane was zooming back and forth, and then circling around and around. As it dipped and turned, it let out a stream of white smoke that wrote a message in the sky.

"Flying *is* fun," thought Goofy. He had always wanted to fly. One time, the wind had tugged so hard at his kite, he had almost believed it would take him up and away.

It hadn't. But up in the sky, he saw people who must have dreamed the same dream, because they had found ways to pretend they were flying. Some of them were parachuting out of a small plane. They wore backpacks that opened up like huge umbrellas and let them float slowly down to the ground.

Other people were hang-gliding, wearing kitelike wings that let them soar through the air like birds.

Goofy took his last ride in a big, beautiful hot-air balloon. He stood in a basket that was attached by ropes to the fat, round balloon. As the balloons around him rose higher and higher, Goofy thought they looked like colored bubbles floating in the sky.

Goofy was so excited by what he'd seen at the Air Fair, he decided to save his money and take a special trip. He made a reservation on a big, fast-flying jumbo jet that would take him to the Kennedy Space Center at Cape Canaveral in Florida. There he could watch a rocket ship take off into space!

At the airport, Goofy waited in the passenger terminal for his flight. He saw people buying tickets and boarding planes. Outside, many different kinds of planes were taking off and landing on the airport runways. From a tall building called the control tower, airport workers directed all the planes as they took off or reached the airport. Goofy could see a big jet coming down to land.

A voice over the loudspeaker called, "Passengers for Flight Number Thirty, please report to the boarding gate."

Goofy looked at his ticket. "Gawrsh," he said. "That's my flight!"

Goofy found his seat. He put on his seat belt and pulled it tight.

In a minute, the powerful engines started to roar. The plane moved down the runway faster and faster until it tilted up and...
lifted off the ground.

The plane ride was as smooth as ice cream. Goofy took a walk in the aisle, ate lunch, and watched a movie. But most of all, he liked looking out the window at the big, blue, endless sky, thinking about how it would feel to be flying off to the moon or past the sun and stars!

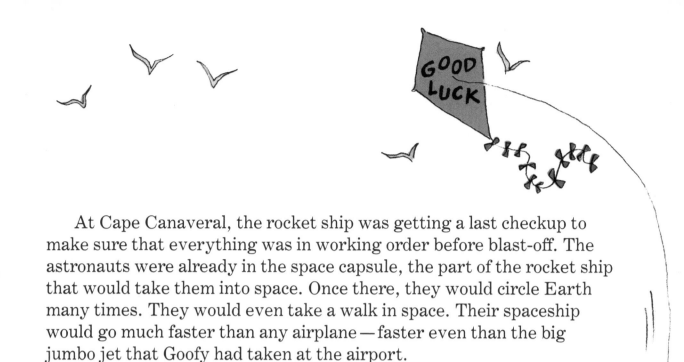

At Cape Canaveral, the rocket ship was getting a last checkup to make sure that everything was in working order before blast-off. The astronauts were already in the space capsule, the part of the rocket ship that would take them into space. Once there, they would circle Earth many times. They would even take a walk in space. Their spaceship would go much faster than any airplane—faster even than the big jumbo jet that Goofy had taken at the airport.

Goofy heard the countdown begin. "Ten-nine-eight-seven-six-five-four-three-two-one. BLAST-OFF!"

As he waved good-bye, Goofy thought, "Maybe someday, I'll fly into space, too!"

And maybe someday, so will you!